Mother Love

MOTHER LOVE

POEMS

Rita Dove

W. W. NORTON & COMPANY
New York   London

The text of this book is composed in Aldus with the display
set in New Rix Fancy, Weiss Initials No. 2, and Baker Signet.
Composition by Crane Typesetting Service, Inc. Manufacturing
by The Collier Companies, Inc. Book design by Charlotte Staub.

ISBN 0-393-03808-4
W. W. Norton & Company, Inc.,
500 Fifth Avenue, New York, N.Y. 10110
W. W. Norton & Company Ltd.,
10 Coptic Street, London WC1A 1PU
1 2 3 4 5 6 7 8 9 0

ACKNOWLEDGMENTS

The poems in *Mother Love* first appeared, sometimes in different versions, in the following periodicals:

American Poetry Review: "Afield," "Demeter, Waiting," "Wiederkehr"; *Atlantic Monthly:* "Used"; *Black Warrior Review:* "Primer," "Party Dress for a First Born," "The Narcissus Flower," "Grief: The Council," "Mother Love," "Breakfast of Champions," "Lamentations," "Nature's Itinerary," "Lost Brilliance"; *Caprice:* "History"; *Callaloo:* "Heroes"; *Georgia Review:* "Statistic: The Witness"; *Gettysburg Review:* "Persephone in Hell"; *High Plains Literary Review:* "The Search" (as "Blown apart . . ."); *Mississippi Review:* "Exit," "Golden Oldie," "Wiring Home"; *Ms. Magazine:* "Persephone Abducted"; *Parnassus:* "The Bistro Styx"; *Ploughshares:* "Missing," "Rusks," "Teotihuacán," "Blue Days" (as "Under Pressure . . ."); *Poetry:* "Demeter Mourning" (as "Sonnet"), "Demeter's Prayer to Hades," "Protection," "Her Island"; *Sequoia:* "Persephone, Falling," "Hades' Pitch" (as "Persephone Underground"); *Sojourner:* "Sonnet in Primary Colors"; *TriQuarterly:* "Political".

An earlier version of the foreword, "An Intact World," was published in *A Formal Feeling Comes—Poems in Form by Contemporary Women*, edited by Annie Finch, Story Line Press, 1994. This anthology also contains the poems "Hades' Pitch" (as "Persephone Underground"), "History," "Political" and "The Search" (as "Blown Apart by Loss . . .").

The opening line to section II of "Persephone in Hell" owes its inspiration to a comment made by Hélène Cixous in a 1982 interview with Verena Andermatt Conley.

The epigraph to section IV is taken from Adrienne Rich's adaptation from the Yiddish of Kadia Molodowsky.

My heartfelt gratitude goes to my husband, Fred Viebahn, for his encouragement and understanding during the composition of these poems. I would like to thank the University of Virginia for its continued support. *Vielen Dank* to Peter Brinkert, Manfred Lisson and Alice Martling, *merci* to Chantal Leib and *thank you* to Julie Fay for assistance in providing space and finding rooms I could temporarily call my own.

FOR
my mother

TO
my daughter

CONTENTS

AN INTACT WORLD

"Sonnet" literally means "little song." The sonnet is a *heile Welt*, an intact world where everything is in sync, from the stars down to the tiniest mite on a blade of grass. And if the "true" sonnet reflects the music of the spheres, it then follows that any variation from the strictly Petrarchan or Shakespearean forms represents a world gone awry.

Or does it? Can't form also be a talisman against disintegration? The sonnet defends itself against the vicissitudes of fortune by its charmed structure, its beautiful bubble. All the while, though, chaos is lurking outside the gate.

The ancient story of Demeter and Persephone is just such a tale of a violated world. It is a modern dilemma as well—there comes a point when a mother can no longer protect her child, when the daughter must go her own way into womanhood. Persephone, out picking flowers with her girl-friends, wanders off from the group. She has just stooped to pluck a golden narcissus, when the earth opens and Hades emerges, dragging her down with him into the Underworld. Inconsolable in her grief, Demeter neglects her duties as goddess of agriculture, and the crops wither. The Olympians disapprove of the abduction but are more shaken by Demeter's reaction, her refusal to return to her godly work in defiance of the laws of nature; she's even left her throne in Olympus and taken to wandering about on earth disguised as a mortal. In varying degrees she is admonished or pitied by the other gods for the depth of her grief. She refuses to accept her fate, however; she strikes out against the Law, forcing Zeus to ask his brother Hades to return Persephone to her mother. Hades agrees.

But ah, can we ever really go back home, as if nothing had happened? Before returning to the surface, the girl eats a few pomegranate seeds, not realizing that anyone who partakes of the food of the dead cannot be wholly restored to the living. So she must spend half of each year at Hades' side, as Queen of the Underworld, and her mother must acquiesce: every fall and winter Demeter is permitted to grieve for the loss of her daughter, letting vegetation wilt and die, but she is obliged to act cheerful in spring and summer, making the earth blossom and bear fruit.

Sonnets seemed the proper mode for most of this work—and not only in homage and as counterpoint to Rilke's *Sonnets to Orpheus*. Much has been said about the many ways to "violate" the sonnet in the service of American speech or modern love or whatever; I will simply say that I like how the sonnet comforts even while its prim borders (but what a pretty fence!) are stultifying; one is constantly bumping up against Order. The Demeter/Persephone cycle of betrayal and regeneration is ideally suited for this form since all three—mother-goddess, daughter-consort and poet—are struggling to sing in their chains.

RITA DOVE

I

One had to choose,
and who would choose the horror?

—JAMES HILLMAN,
The Dream and the Underworld

Heroes

A flower in a weedy field:
make it a poppy. You pick it.
Because it begins to wilt

you run to the nearest house
to ask for a jar of water.
The woman on the porch starts

screaming: you've plucked the last poppy
in her miserable garden, the one
that gave her the strength every morning

to rise! It's too late for apologies
though you go through the motions, offering
trinkets and a juicy spot in the written history

she wouldn't live to read, anyway.
So you strike her, she hits
her head on a white boulder,

and there's nothing to be done
but break the stone into gravel
to prop up the flower in the stolen jar

you have to take along,
because you're a fugitive now
and you can't leave clues.

Already the story's starting to unravel,
the villagers stirring as your heart
pounds into your throat. O why

did you pick that idiot flower?
Because it was the last one
and you knew

it was going to die.

II

Baby, baby, if he hears you
As he gallops past the house,
Limb from limb at once he'll tear you,
Just as pussy tears a mouse.

And he'll beat you, beat you, beat you,
And he'll beat you all to pap,
And he'll eat you, eat you, eat you,
Every morsel snap, snap, snap.

—Mother Goose

Primer

In the sixth grade I was chased home by
the Gatlin kids, three skinny sisters
in rolled-down bobby socks. Hissing
Brainiac! and *Mrs. Stringbean!*, they trod my heel.
I knew my body was no big deal
but never thought to retort: who's
calling *who* skinny? (Besides, I knew
they'd beat me up.) I survived
their shoves across the schoolyard
because my five-foot-zero mother drove up
in her Caddie to shake them down to size.
Nothing could get me into that car.
I took the long way home, swore
I'd show them all: I would grow up.

Party Dress for a First Born

Headless girl so ill at ease on the bed,
I know, if you could, what you're thinking of:
nothing. I used to think that, too,
whenever I sat down to a full plate
or unwittingly stepped on an ant.
When I ran to my mother, waiting radiant
as a cornstalk at the edge of the field,
nothing else mattered: the world stood still.

Tonight men stride like elegant scissors across the lawn
to the women arrayed there, petals waiting to loosen.
When I step out, disguised in your blushing skin,
they will nudge each other to get a peek
and I will smile, all the while wishing them dead.
Mother's calling. Stand up: it will be our secret.

Persephone, Falling

One narcissus among the ordinary beautiful
flowers, one unlike all the others! She pulled,
stooped to pull harder—
when, sprung out of the earth
on his glittering terrible
carriage, he claimed his due.
It is finished. No one heard her.
No one! She had strayed from the herd.

(Remember: go straight to school.
This is important, stop fooling around!
Don't answer to strangers. Stick
with your playmates. Keep your eyes down.)
This is how easily the pit
opens. This is how one foot sinks into the ground.

The Search

Blown apart by loss, she let herself go—
wandered the neighborhood hatless, breasts
swinging under a ratty sweater, crusted
mascara blackening her gaze. It was a shame,
the wives whispered, to carry on so.
To them, wearing foam curlers arraigned
like piglets to market was almost debonair,
but an uncombed head?—not to be trusted.

The men watched more closely, tantalized
by so much indifference. Winter came early and still
she frequented the path by the river until
one with murmurous eyes pulled her down to size.
Sniffed Mrs. Franklin, ruling matron, to the rest:
Serves her right, the old mare.

Protection

Are you having a good time?
Are you having a time at all?
Everywhere in the garden I see the slim vine
of your neck, the stubborn baby curls . . .

I know I'm not saying this right.
"Good" hair has no body
in this country; like trained ivy,
it hangs and shines. Mine comes out

in clusters. Is there such
a thing as a warning? The Hawaiian
mulberry is turning to ash

and the snail has lost its home.
Are you really all over with? How done
is gone?

The Narcissus Flower

I remember my foot in its frivolous slipper,
a frightened bird . . . not the earth unzipped

but the way I could see my own fingers and hear
myself scream as the blossom incinerated.

And though nothing could chasten
the plunge, this man
adamant as a knife easing into

the humblest crevice, I found myself at
the center of a calm so pure, it was hate.

The mystery is, you can eat fear
before fear eats you,

you can live beyond dying—
and become a queen
whom nothing surprises.

Persephone Abducted

She cried out for Mama, who did not
hear. She left with a wild eye thrown back,
she left with curses, rage
that withered her features to a hag's.
No one can tell a mother how to act:
there are no laws when laws are broken, no names
to call upon. Some say there's nourishment for pain,

and call it Philosophy.
That's for the birds, vulture and hawk,
the large ones who praise
the miracle of flight because
they use it so diligently.
She left us singing in the field, oblivious
to all but the ache of our own bent backs.

Statistic: The Witness

No matter where I turn, she is there
screaming. No matter how
I run, pause to catch a breath—
until I am the one screaming
as the drone of an engine overtakes
the afternoon.

I know I should stop looking, do
as my mother says—turn my head
to the wall and tell Jesus—but
I keep remembering things,
clearer and smaller: his watch,
his wrist, the two ashen ovals
etched on her upturned sandals.

Now I must walk this faithless earth
which cannot readjust an abyss
into flowering meadow.
I will walk until I reach
green oblivion . . . then
I will lie down in its kindness,
in the bottomless lull of her arms.

Grief: The Council

I told her: enough is enough.
Get a hold on yourself, take a lover,
help some other unfortunate child.

> *to abdicate*
> *to let the garden go to seed*

Yes it's a tragedy, a low-down shame,
but you still got your own life to live. Meanwhile,
ain't nothing we can do but be discreet
and wait. She brightened up a bit, then.
I thought of those blurred snapshots framed
on milk cartons, a new pair each week.

> *soot drifting up from hell*
> *dusting the kale's*
> *green tresses, the corn's green sleeve*

It was pathetic. I bet she ain't took in
a word I said except that last, like
a dog with a chicken bone too greedy to care
if it stick in his gullet and choke him sure.

> *and no design*

I say we gotta see her through.
I say she can't be left too long in that
drafty old house alone.

> *no end-of-day delight*
> *at the creak of the gate*

15

Sister Jeffries, you could drop in
tomorrow morning, take one
of your Mason jars, something
sweetish, tomatoes or bell peppers.

> *no tender cheek nor ripening grape*
> *destined for wine*

Miz Earl can fetch her later to the movies—
a complicated plot should distract her,
something with a car chase through Manhattan,
loud horns melting to a strings-and-sax ending

> *the last frail tendril snapped free*
> *(though the roots still strain toward her)*

and your basic sunshine pouring through
the clouds. Ain't this crazy weather?
Feels like winter coming on.

> *at last the earth cleared to the sea*
> *at last composure*

Mother Love

Who can forget the attitude of mothering?
       Toss me a baby and without bothering
to blink I'll catch her, sling him on a hip.
       Any woman knows the remedy for grief
is being needed: duty bugles and we'll
       climb out of exhaustion every time,
bare the nipple or tuck in the sheet,
       heat milk and hum at bedside until
they can dress themselves and rise, primed
       for Love or Glory—those one-way mirrors
girls peer into as their fledgling heroes slip
       through, storming the smoky battlefield.

So when this kind woman approached at the urging
       of her bouquet of daughters,
(one for each of the world's corners,
       one for each of the winds to scatter!)
and offered up her only male child for nursing
       (a smattering of flesh, noisy and ordinary),
I put aside the lavish trousseau of the mourner
       for the daintier comfort of pity:
I decided to save him. Each night
       I laid him on the smoldering embers,
sealing his juices in slowly so he might
       be cured to perfection. Oh, I know it
looked damning: at the hearth a muttering crone
       bent over a baby sizzling on a spit
as neat as a Virginia ham. Poor human—
       to scream like that, to make me remember.

Breakfast of Champions

Finally, overcast skies. I've crossed a hemisphere,
worked my way through petals and sunlight
to find a place fit for mourning,
a little dust on the laurel branch.
I'll dive into a grateful martini tonight,
eye to eye with the olive adrift in cool ether—
but for now, here's weather to match
my condition: the first pair of Canada geese

have arrived on the lake. I rummage the pantry's
stock for raisins and cereal as they pull
honking out of the mist, a sonic hospital graph
announcing recovery. Arise, it's a brand new morning!
Though I pour myself the recommended bowlful,
stones are what I sprinkle among the chaff.

Golden Oldie

I made it home early, only to get
stalled in the driveway, swaying
at the wheel like a blind pianist caught in a tune
meant for more than two hands playing.

The words were easy, crooned
by a young girl dying to feel alive, to discover
a pain majestic enough
to live by. I turned the air-conditioning off,

leaned back to float on a film of sweat,
and listened to her sentiment:
Baby, where did our love go?—a lament
I greedily took in

without a clue who my lover
might be, or where to start looking.

III

Who can escape life, fever,
the darkness of the abyss?
lost, lost, lost . . .

    H.D., *Hermetic Definition*

Persephone in Hell

I.

I was not quite twenty when I first went down
into the stone chasms of the City of Lights,
every morning four flights creaking under my rubber soles.
At the end of each dim hall, a tiny window tipped
toward the clouds admitted light into
those loveless facilities shared by
the shameful poor and the shamelessly young.
Girded, then, with youth and good tennis shoes,
I climbed down guided
by the smell of bread,
the reek of multiplying yeast.
With my seven words of French,
with my exact change I walked
the storefronts where the double-plated
windows were as coolly arranged
as a spray of bridesmaids:
bazooka sausages, fields of silk,
"ladies' foundations" in winch-and-pulley configurations,

and at last, squadrons of baked goods:
croissants glazed in the sheen of desire,
the sweating dark caps of the *têtes au nègres*,
nipples gleaming on the innocent *beignets*;
I surveyed them, each in its majesty,
and stepped over the tinkling threshold,
instantly foreign: *une baguette et*
cinq croissants beurre, s'il vous plaît.
There were five of us, five girls.

Banknote and silver
crossed palms and I was outside again,
awash in a rush of Peugeots and honking
delivery vans.

For a moment I forgot which way to turn,
what the month was, the reason for
my high-pitched vigilance—
then it came back: turn left, cross
the avenue, dodge poodle shit
and tsking nannies. It was October.
Sweat faded into the terried insteps
of my miraculous American sneakers
while the sour ecstasy of bread
(its chaste white wrapper rustling,
the brown heel broken off)
calmed me.

II.

It's an old drama, waiting.
One grows into it,
enough to fill the boredom . . .
it's a treacherous fit.

Mother worried. Mother with her frilly ideals
gave me money to call home every day,
but she couldn't know what I was feeling;
I was doing what she didn't need to know.
I was doing everything and feeling nothing.

corn in the husk
vine unfurling

Autumn soured. Little lace-up boots
appeared on the heels of shopkeepers
while their clientele sported snappier versions;
black parabolas of balcony grills
echoed in their three-inch heels.

my dove   my snail

Two days of rain, how to spend them?
Clip on large earrings, man's sweater, black tights;
walk an old umbrella through the passage
at number 17, dip in for *chocolat chaud*
while watching the Africans
fold up their straw mats and wooden beads.

There was love, of course. Mostly boys:
a flat-faced engineering student from Missouri,
a Texan flaunting his teaspoon of Cherokee blood.

I waited for afterwards—their pale eyelids, foreheads
thrown back so the rapture could evaporate.
I don't believe I was suffering. I was curious,
    mainly:
How would each one smell, how many ways could
    he do it?
I was drowning in flowers.

III.

I visited a former schoolmate who'd married
onto the Île—a two-room attic walk-up
crammed with mahogany heirlooms,
but just lean over the offensive tin sink in the kitchen
and there she was, Our Lady, crusty with gargoyles.
The party they threw for Armistice Day
was cocktails with bad sculpture,
listening for meaningful conversation
among expatriate Americans lounging against the
    upright coffins.

    - How're you liking it so far? I admit, you
    gotta dodge shit every place you look.
    - What about them little white poodles
    stamped on sidewalks everywhere? Aren't
    they meant for curbing?
    - Yeah, but Parisians love their dogs too
    much. Besides, Parisians don't mind dog
    shit because it's not their shit, you see; it
    makes them feel superior.

    are you having a good time
    are you having a time at all

There were crudités, peanuts. Banjos appeared, spilling
zeal like popcorn. I decided to let this party
swing without me.

IV.

Cross the Seine, avoid Our Lady's
crepuscular shadow. Chill at my back.

> *Which way is bluer?*

One round of Boul' Mich: bookstore, kiosk,
heat blast from the metro pit. Down, then.

> *And if I refuse this being*
> *which way then?*

Three stops, out: moonlit façade
of the *Marais*, spun-sugar stucco and iron filigree:
a retinue of little dramas
tucked in for the night.

Through the gutters, dry rivers
of the season's detritus.
Wind soughing the plane trees.
I command my knees to ignore the season
as I scuttle over stones, marking pace
by the intermittent evidence of canine
love: heaped droppings scored with frost.

Near Beaubourg, even the air twitters.
Racks of T-shirts cut from
inferior cloth, postcard stands, all
the assumed élan and bric-a-brac
dissolves with a turn
that pitches me onto the concrete brim
of the Centre Pompidou.

Mon Dieu, the wind!
My head fills with ice.

　　　　　　This is how the pit opens

Sheared of its proletarian stubble
(brothels and cheap hotels),
this bulldozed amphitheater
catches the iron breath of winter, sending
tourist and *clochard* into the breach,
dachshund and snapped umbrella,
each stubborn leaf and exiled twig
swirling into whatever that is
down there, throbbing with neon tubing
like some demented plumber's diagram
of a sinner's soul—

　　　　　　This is how one foot
　　　　　　sinks into the ground

V.

God, humans are a noisy zoo—
especially educated ones armed with *vin rouge*
and an incomprehensible no-act play.

The crush, the unbearable stench!
They insist on overheating these affairs,
as if to remind the leftist bourgeoisie
just who wove those welcome mats
they wipe their combat boots on.
Rad Chic: black corduroy and
leather vests. The saints were right
to flog the body, or starve it into heaven.

I need a *divertissement*:
The next one through that gate,
woman or boy, will get
the full-court press of my ennui.

Merde,
too many at once! Africans,
spilling up the escalator
like oil from lucky soil—

let me get my rules straight.
Should I count them as singular
plural, like popcorn?
Or can I wait for one person
to separate from the crowd,
chin lifted for courage, as if to place
her brave, lost countenance
under my care . . .

Contact.

VI.

After the wind, this air
imploded down my throat,
a hot, rank syrup swirled with smoke
from a hundred cigarettes.
Soft chatter roaring. French nothings.
I don't belong here.

> She doesn't belong, that's certain.
> Leather skirt's slipped
> a bit: sweet. No gloves? American,
> because she wears black badly.
> I'd like to see her in chartreuse,
> walking around like a living
> after-dinner drink.

He inclines his head, rather massive,
like a cynical parrot. Almost a smile.

> *"Puis-je vous offrir mes services?"*

Sotto voce, his inquiry
curls down to lick my hand.
Standard nicety, probably,
but my French could not stand up
to meet it.

> *"Or myself, if you are looking."*
> I whisper this. I'm sure she doesn't understand.

"Pardon me?"

> *"Excuse, I thought you were French.
> You are looking for someone?"*

31

"Yes. I'm . . . sure he's here somewhere."
Here you are.

          "I hope he won't let himself
          be found too soon. A drink?"

He's gone and back, as easily as smoke,
in each hand a slim glass
alive with a brilliant lime.
"What time is it?"

          she blurts,
          shrinking from the glass.
          "*À minuit.* Midnight.
          The zero hour,
          you call it?"

Again the dark smile.
"Some call it that."

          "Chartreuse," I say, holding out a glass,
          "is a tint not to be found *au naturel*
          in all of France, except in bottles
          and certain days at the Côte d'Azur
          when sun performs on ocean what
          we call *un mirage,* a—"

"trick of light." I take the glass,
lift it to meet his.

VII.

if I whispered to the moon

                                    I am waiting

if I whispered to the olive

                                    you are on the way

which would hear me?

                                    I am listening

the garden gone

                                    the seed in darkness

the city around me

                                    I am waiting

it was cold I entered

                                    you rise into my arms

I entered for warmth

                                    I part the green sheaths

a part of me had been waiting

                                    I part the brown field

already in this cold longing

                                    and you are sinking

who has lost me?

                                    through heat the whispers

be still, mother whispers

                                    through whispers the sighing

and let sorrow travel

                                    through sighing the darkness

be still she whispers

                                    I am waiting

and light will enter

                                    you are on your way

IV

On and on my mother would go. No small part of my life was so unimportant that she hadn't made a note of it, and now she would tell it to me over and over again.

—JAMAICA KINCAID,
"The Circling Hand"

Hades' Pitch

If I could just touch your ankle, he whispers, *there
on the inside, above the bone*—leans closer,
breath of lime and peppers—*I know I could
make love to you.* She considers
this, secretly thrilled, though she wasn't quite
sure what he meant. He was good
with words, words that went straight to the liver.
Was she falling for him out of sheer boredom—
cooped up in this anything-but-humble dive, stone
gargoyles leering and brocade drapes licked with fire?
Her ankle burns where he described it. She sighs
just as her mother aboveground stumbles, is caught
by the fetlock—bereft in an instant—
while the Great Man drives home his desire.

Wiederkehr

He only wanted me for happiness:
to walk in air
and not think so much,
to watch the smile
begun in his eyes
end on the lips
his eyes caressed.

He merely hoped, in darkness, to smell
rain; and though he saw how still
I sat to hold the rain untouched
inside me, he never asked
if I would stay. Which is why,
when the choice appeared,
I reached for it.

Wiring Home

Lest the wolves loose their whistles
and shopkeepers inquire,

keep moving; though your knees flush
red as two chapped apples,

keep moving, head up,
past the beggar's cold cup,

past fires banked under chestnuts
and the trumpeting kiosk's

tales of odyssey and heartbreak
until, turning a corner, you stand

staring: ambushed
by a window of canaries

bright as a thousand
golden narcissi.

The Bistro Styx

She was thinner, with a mannered gauntness
as she paused just inside the double
glass doors to survey the room, silvery cape
billowing dramatically behind her. *What's this,*

I thought, lifting a hand until
she nodded and started across the parquet;
that's when I saw she was dressed all in gray,
from a kittenish cashmere skirt and cowl

down to the graphite signature of her shoes.
"Sorry I'm late," she panted, though
she wasn't, sliding into the chair, her cape

tossed off in a shudder of brushed steel.
We kissed. Then I leaned back to peruse
my blighted child, this wary aristocratic mole.

"How's business?" I asked, and hazarded
a motherly smile to keep from crying out:
Are you content to conduct your life
as a cliché and, what's worse,

an anachronism, the brooding artist's demimonde?
Near the rue Princesse they had opened
a gallery *cum* souvenir shop which featured
fuzzy off-color Monets next to his acrylics, no doubt,

plus bearded African drums and the occasional miniature
gargoyle from Notre Dame the Great Artist had
carved at breakfast with a pocket knife.

"Tourists love us. The Parisians, of course"—
she blushed—"are amused, though not without
a certain admiration . . ."
                              The Chateaubriand

arrived on a bone-white plate, smug and absolute
in its fragrant crust, a black plug steaming
like the heart plucked from the chest of a worthy enemy;
one touch with her fork sent pink juices streaming.

"Admiration for what?" Wine, a bloody
Pinot Noir, brought color to her cheeks. "Why,
the aplomb with which we've managed
to support our Art"—meaning he'd convinced

her to pose nude for his appalling canvases,
faintly futuristic landscapes strewn
with carwrecks and bodies being chewed

by rabid cocker spaniels. "I'd like to come by
the studio," I ventured, "and see the new stuff."
"Yes, if you wish . . ." A delicate rebuff

before the warning: "He dresses all
in black now. Me, he drapes in blues and carmine—
and even though I think it's kinda cute,
in company I tend toward more muted shades."

She paused and had the grace
to drop her eyes. She did look ravishing,
spookily insubstantial, a lipstick ghost on tissue,
or as if one stood on a fifth-floor terrace

peering through a fringe of rain at Paris'
dreaming chimney pots, each sooty issue
wobbling skyward in an ecstatic oracular spiral.

"And he never thinks of food. I wish
I didn't have to plead with him to eat. . . ." Fruit
and cheese appeared, arrayed on leaf-green dishes.

I stuck with café crème. "This Camembert's
so ripe," she joked, "it's practically grown hair,"
mucking a golden glob complete with parsley sprig
onto a heel of bread. Nothing seemed to fill

her up: She swallowed, sliced into a pear,
speared each tear-shaped lavaliere
and popped the dripping mess into her pretty mouth.
Nowhere the bright tufted fields, weighted

vines and sun poured down out of the south.
"But are you happy?" Fearing, I whispered it
quickly. "What? You know, Mother"—

she bit into the starry rose of a fig—
"one really should try the fruit here."
I've lost her, I thought, and called for the bill.

V

Tighten the sails of night as far as you can,
for the daylight cannot carry me.

KADIA MOLODOWSKY,
"White Night"

Blue Days

Under pressure Mick tells me one
of the jokes truckers pass among themselves: *Why
do women have legs?* I can't imagine;
the day is too halcyon, beyond the patio too Arizonan
blue, sparrows drunk on figs and the season's first corn
stacked steaming on the wicker table. . . . *I
give up; why do they?* As if I weren't one
of "them." Nothing surpasses these
kernels, taut-to-bursting sweet,
tiny rows translucent as baby teeth.
Remember, you asked for it:
to keep them from tracking slime over the floor.

Demeter, here's another one for your basket
of mysteries.

Nature's Itinerary

Irene says it's the altitude
that makes my period late;
this time, though, it's eluded
me entirely. I shouldn't worry (I'm medically regulated)
—but hell, I brought these thirty sanitary pads
all the way from Köln to Mexico, prepared
for more than metaphorical bloodletting among the glad rags
of the Festival Internacional de Poesia,
and I forbid
my body to be so cavalier.
Taking the pill is like using a safety net
but then, beforehand, having a beer—
a man's invention to numb us so we
can't tell which way the next wind's blowing.

Sonnet in Primary Colors

This is for the woman with one black wing
perched over her eyes: lovely Frida, erect
among parrots, in the stern petticoats of the peasant,
who painted herself a present—
wildflowers entwining the plaster corset
her spine resides in, that flaming pillar—
this priestess in the romance of mirrors.

Each night she lay down in pain and rose
to the celluloid butterflies of her Beloved Dead,
Lenin and Marx and Stalin arrayed at the footstead.
And rose to her easel, the hundred dogs panting
like children along the graveled walks of the garden, Diego's
love a skull in the circular window
of the thumbprint searing her immutable brow.

Demeter Mourning

Nothing can console me. You may bring silk
to make skin sigh, dispense yellow roses
in the manner of ripened dignitaries.
You can tell me repeatedly
I am unbearable (and I know this):
still, nothing turns the gold to corn,
nothing is sweet to the tooth crushing in.

I'll not ask for the impossible;
one learns to walk by walking.
In time I'll forget this empty brimming,
I may laugh again at
a bird, perhaps, chucking the nest—
but it will not be happiness,
for I have known that.

Exit

Just when hope withers, a reprieve is granted.
The door opens onto a street like in the movies,
clean of people, of cats; except it is *your* street
you are leaving. Reprieve has been granted,
"provisionally"—a fretful word.

The windows you have closed behind
you are turning pink, doing what they do
every dawn. Here it's gray; the door
to the taxicab waits. This suitcase,
the saddest object in the world.

Well, the world's open. And now through
the windshield the sky begins to blush,
as you did when your mother told you
what it took to be a woman in this life.

Afield

Out where crows dip to their kill
under the clouds' languid white oars
she wanders, hands pocketed, hair combed tight
so she won't feel the breeze quickening—
as if she were trying to get back to him,
find the breach in the green
that would let her slip through,
then tug meadow over the wound like a sheet.

I've walked there, too: he can't give
you up, so you give in until you can't live
without him. Like these blossoms, white sores
burst upon earth's ignorant flesh, at first sight
everything is innocence—
then it's itch, scratch, putrescence.

Lost Brilliance

I miss that corridor drenched in shadow,
sweat of centuries steeped into stone.
After the plunge, after my shrieks
diminished and his oars sighed
up to the smoking shore,
the bulwark's gray pallor soothed me.
Even the columns seemed kind, their murky sheen
like the lustrous skin of a roving eye.

I used to stand at the top of the stair
where the carpet flung down
its extravagant heart. Flames
teased the lake into glimmering licks.
I could pretend to be above the earth
rather than underground: a Venetian
palazzo or misty chalet tucked into
an Alp, that mixture of comfort
and gloom . . . nothing was simpler

to imagine. But it was more difficult
each evening to descend: all that marble
flayed with the red plush of privilege
I traveled on, slow nautilus
unwinding in terrified splendor
to where he knew to meet me—
my consort, my match,
though much older and sadder.

In time, I lost the capacity
for resolve. It was as if
I had been traveling all these years
without a body,
until his hands found me—
and then there was just
the two of us forever:
one who wounded,
and one who served.

VI

Now, for the first time, the god lifts his hand,
the fragments join in me with their own music.

—MURIEL RUKEYSER,
"The Poem as Mask"

Political

(for Breyten Breytenbach)

There was a man spent seven years in hell's circles—
no moon or starlight, shadows singing
their way to slaughter. We give him honorary status.
There's a way to study freedom but few have found
it; you must talk yourself to death and then beyond,
destroy time, then refashion it. Even Demeter keeps digging
towards that darkest miracle,
the hope of finding her child unmolested.

This man did something ill advised, for good reason.
(I mean he went about it wrong.)
And paid in shit, the world is shit and shit
can make us grown. It is becoming the season
she was taken from us. Our wail starts up
of its own accord, is mistaken for song.

Demeter, Waiting

No. Who can bear it. Only someone
who hates herself, who believes
to pull a hand back from a daughter's cheek
is to put love into her pocket—
like one of those ashen Christian
philosophers, or a war-bound soldier.

She is gone again and I will not bear
it, I will drag my grief through a winter
of my own making and refuse
any meadow that recycles itself into
hope. Shit on the cicadas, dry meteor
flash, finicky butterflies! I will wail and thrash
until the whole goddamned golden panorama freezes
over. Then I will sit down to wait for her. Yes.

Lamentations

Throw open the shutters
to your darkened residences:
can you hear the pipes playing,
their hunger shaking the olive branches?
To hear them sighing and not answer
is to deny this world, descend rung
by rung into no loss and no desire.
Listen: empty yet full, silken
air and brute tongue,
they are saying:
To refuse to be born is one thing—
but once you are here,
you'd do well to stop crying
and suck the good milk in.

Teotihuacán

The Indian guide explains to the group of poets
how the Aztec slaves found parasites in cocoons
spun like snowdrifts around the spinules
of a cactus pad (his aide scrapes some free with a stick)
and ground them to a fine red paste.
Next, an unassuming stalk which, chewed,
produced a showy green (a younger stalk
made yellow) and these they used
to decorate the Temple of the Sun.
Plumed serpent who reared his head in the east,
his watery body everywhere: Quetzalcoatl
was a white man, blond hair and tall.
It took millions of these bugs to stain a single wall.
The poets scribble in assorted notebooks. The guide moves on.

History

Everything's a metaphor, some wise
guy said, and his woman nodded, wisely.
Why was this such a discovery
to him? Why did history
happen only on the outside?
She'd watched an embryo track an arc
across her swollen belly from the inside
and knew she'd best
think *knee*, not *tumor* or *burrowing mole*, lest
it emerge a monster. Each craving marks
the soul: splashed white upon a temple the dish
of ice cream, coveted, broken in a wink,
or the pickle duplicated just behind the ear. *Every wish
will find its symbol,* the woman thinks.

Used

The conspiracy's to make us thin. Size threes
are all the rage, and skirts ballooning above twinkling knees
are every man-child's preadolescent dream.
Tabula rasa. No slate's *that* clean—

we've earned the navels sunk in grief
when the last child emptied us of their brief
interior light. Our muscles say *We have been used.*

Have you ever tried silk sheets? I did,
persuaded by postnatal dread
and a Macy's clerk to bargain for more zip.
We couldn't hang on, slipped
to the floor and by morning the quilts
had slid off, too. Enough of guilt—
It's hard work staying cool.

Rusks

This is how it happened.

Spring wore on my nerves—
all that wheezing and dripping
while others in galoshes
reaped compost and seemed
enamored most of the time.

Why should I be select?

I got tired of tearing myself down.
Let someone else have
the throne of blues for a while,
let someone else suffer mosquitoes.
As my mama always said:
half a happiness is better
than none at goddam all.

Missing

I am the daughter who went out with the girls,
never checked back in and nothing marked my "last
known whereabouts," not a single glistening petal.

Horror is partial; it keeps you going. A lost
child is a fact hardening around its absence,
a knot in the breast purring *Touch, and I will*

come true. I was "returned," I watched her
watch as I babbled *It could have been worse. . . .*
Who can tell
what penetrates? Pity is the brutal
discipline. Now I understand she can never
die, just as nothing can bring me back—

I am the one who comes and goes;
I am the footfall that hovers.

Demeter's Prayer to Hades

This alone is what I wish for you: knowledge.
To understand each desire has an edge,
to know we are responsible for the lives
we change. No faith comes without cost,
no one believes without dying.
Now for the first time
I see clearly the trail you planted,
what ground opened to waste,
though you dreamed a wealth
of flowers.

             There are no curses—only mirrors
held up to the souls of gods and mortals.
And so I give up this fate, too.
Believe in yourself,
go ahead—see where it gets you.

VII

Is this the Region, this the Soil, the Clime
Said then the lost Arch Angel, this the seat
That we must change for Heav'n, this mournful glow
For that celestial light?

—JOHN MILTON,
Paradise Lost

Her Island

the heat, the stench of things,
the unutterable boredom of it all . . .

—H.D., *Notes on Thought and Vision*

Around us: blazed stones, closed ground.
Waiters lounge, stricken with sirocco,
ice cream disintegrates to a sticky residue
fit for flies and ants. Summer, the dead season.
All the temples of Agrigento
line up like a widow's extracted wisdom teeth:
ocher-stained, proud remnants
of the last sturdy thing about her.

We wander among orange peels and wax
wrappings flecked with grease,
tilt our guidebook, pages blank from sun, and peer
up into the bottomless air. Between columns,
blue slashes of a torched heaven. No,
let it go: nothing will come of this.

Let it go: nothing will come of this
textbook rampaging, though we have found, by
stint and intuition, the chthonic grotto,
closed for the season behind a chicken-wire gate.
We're too well trained to trespass. Clearly
we can imagine what's beyond it. Clearly
we've sought succor in the wrong corner.
Nothing melts faster than resolve in this climate;
we turn to a funny man in our path, old
as everything is here is either old
or scathingly young with whippet thighs
clamped over a souped-up Vespa. *You wish
to visit historic site?* We nod, politely;
he shuffles off to find the key.

He shuffles off to find the key,
dust blooming between us to obscure
what we had missed on the way in:
at the head of the path a shack
the size of an outhouse from which he now emerges
hobbling, Quasimodo in a sunnier vein.

An eternity at the rusted lock, then down. It's noon:
we must be madder than the English
with their dogs. Look at his shoes,
he's trod them into slippers!
His touch trembles at my arm;
hasn't he seen an American Black
before? We find a common language: German.

Before we find a common language—German,
laced with tenth-grade Spanish and
residual Latin—we descend
in silence through the parched orchard.
The way he stops to smile at me
and pat my arm, I'm surely his first
Queen of Sheba.

        The grotto is
a disappointment, as every site has been
so far. Isn't there a way to tip him early
and get the hell back to the car?
Insulting an old man just isn't done.
Nothing to do but help him conjugate
his verbs and smile until our cheeks ache,
our hands admiring every grimy stone.

Our hands admiring every grimy stone,
we let our minds drift far afield:
there's a miracle, a lone bird
singing. What's that
he's saying? *Krieg*? Stilted
German, gathered word by word
half a century ago. I shudder

as he motions my husband close, man to man:
would he like to see a true wonder?
No, not dirty. Another temple, overgrown,
lost to busy people—he mimics Fiats
zipping by—a man's shrine, the god
of fire. Ah, Vulcan? Emphatic nod.
He's had the key for many years, they've all forgotten.

He's had the key for many years; they've all forgotten
the ugly god, god of all that's modern.
We toil cross-town, down ever-dwindling streets
until we're certain we're about to turn into
the latest victims of a tourist scam. A sharp curve
under the *autostrada* confirms the destiny
we at least should meet head on: we climb
straight through the city dump,
through rotten fruit and Tampax tubes
so our treacherous guide can deliver us into

what couldn't be: a patch of weeds sprouting six—no, seven—
columns, their Doric reserve softened by weather
to tawny indifference. Roosters cluck among the ruins;
traffic whizzes by in heaven.

Traffic whizzes by in heaven
for the Sicilians, of that we're certain;
why else are they practicing on earth, hell-bent
to overtake creampuff foreigners in their rented
Chrysler? Ha! Can't they guess a German
plies the wheel? We dash along beside
them, counterclockwise around the island,
not looking for the ironies we see in spades—
Palermo's golden virgin carried down to sea
as a car bomb blows a judge to smoke,
five brides whose lacquered faces echo those
ones staring, self-mocking, from lurid frescoes
at the Villa Casale: *an eye for an eye.* And
everywhere temples, or pieces of them.

Everywhere temples, or pieces of them,
lay scattered across the countryside.
These monstrous broken sticks, flung
aside in a celestial bout of I Ching, have become
Sicily's most exalted litter. (The lesser kind
flies out the windows of honking automobiles.)

We circle the island, trailing the sun
on his daily rounds, turning time back
to one infernal story: a girl
pulled into a lake, one perfect oval
hemmed all around by reeds
at the center of the physical world.
We turn inland as if turning a page in a novel:
dry splash of the cicada, no breath from the sea.

Dry splash of the cicada, no breath from the sea.
Our maps have not failed us: this is it,
the only body of water for twenty miles,
water black and still as the breath
it harbored; and around this perfect ellipse
they've built . . . a racetrack.

Bleachers. Pit stops. A ten-foot fence
plastered with ads—Castrol, Campari—
and looped barbed wire; no way to get near.
We drive the circumference
with binoculars: no cave, no reeds.
We drive it twice, first one way, then back,
to cancel our rage at the human need
to make a sport of death.

To make a sport of death
it must be endless: round and round
till you feel everything you've trained for—
precision, speed, endurance—reduced to this
godawful roar, this vale of sound.

Your head's a furnace: you don't feel it.
Your eyes, two slits in a computer unit.
A vital rule: if two vehicles ahead of you
crash, drive straight toward the fire
and they will have veered away before you get
there. Bell lap, don't look to see who's
gaining. Aim for the tape, aim *through* it.
Then rip the helmet off and poke your head
through sunlight, into flowers.

Through sunlight into flowers
she walked, and was pulled down.
A simple story, a mother's deepest
dread—that her child could drown
in sweetness.

                Where the chariot went under
no one can fathom. Water keeps its horrors
while Sky proclaims his, hangs them
in stars. Only Earth—wild
mother we can never leave (even now
we've leaned against her, heads bowed
against the heat)—knows
no story's ever finished; it just goes
on, unnoticed in the dark that's all
around us: blazed stones, the ground closed.

About the Author

Rita Dove served as Poet Laureate of the United States and Consultant in Poetry at the Library of Congress from 1993 to 1995. Born in 1952 in Akron, Ohio, she has published five poetry collections, among them *Thomas and Beulah,* which was awarded the Pulitzer Prize in 1987. She is also the author of a book of short stories, the novel *Through the Ivory Gate* and the verse play *The Darker Face of the Earth;* its stage premiere is planned for 1996.

Ms. Dove's honors include Fulbright, Guggenheim and Mellon fellowships, grants from the National Endowment for the Arts and the National Endowment for the Humanities, as well as residencies at Tuskegee Institute, the National Humanities Center and the Rockefeller Foundation's Villa Serbelloni in Bellagio, Italy. Robert Penn Warren chose her for the Academy of American Poets' Lavan Award shortly after he was named the first U.S. Poet Laureate in 1986. Ms. Dove is also the recipient of a General Electric Foundation Award, several honorary doctorates, a Literary Lion citation from the New York Public Library, the NAACP Great American Artist Award, the Golden Plate Award from the American Academy of Achievement, the Folger Shakespeare Library's Renaissance Forum Award for leadership in the literary arts, *Glamour* magazine's "Women of the Year" Award, and many other recognitions. In 1993 she became the first poet in more than a decade to give an official poetry reading at the White House.

Rita Dove is Commonwealth Professor of English at the University of Virginia. She lives near Charlottesville, Virginia, with her husband and daughter.